Sea Level Rising

SEA LEVEL
RISING

POEMS BY
John Philip Drury

ABLE MUSE PRESS

Copyright ©2015 by John Philip Drury
First published in 2015 by

Able Muse Press

www.ablemusepress.com

All rights reserved. No part of this book may be used or reproduced in any manner whatsoever without written permission except in the case of brief quotations embedded in critical articles and reviews. Requests for permission should be addressed to the Able Muse Press editor at editor@ablemuse.com

Printed in the United States of America

Library of Congress Control Number: 2014950255

ISBN 978-1-927409-42-8 (paperback)
ISBN 978-1-927409-41-1 (digital)

Cover image: "Big Wind" by Robert Tharsing, oil on panel, 19 1/2" x 25 3/4", 2005

Cover & book design by Alexander Pepple

Able Muse Press is an imprint of *Able Muse:* A Review of Poetry, Prose & Art—at www.ablemuse.com

Able Muse Press
467 Saratoga Avenue #602
San Jose, CA 95129

for LaWanda

Curse on all laws but those which love has made!
 —Alexander Pope, "Eloisa to Abelard"

Acknowledgments

I am grateful to the editors of the following journals where many of these poems originally appeared, sometimes in earlier versions:

Able Muse: "Ghazal of the Lutanist," "Girl on a Fishing Boat," "Song with a Bridge."
The Antioch Review: "Coastal Warning Displays."
Ascent: "Crossing the Lagoon."
The Baltimore Review: "How to Stay Awake."
Cincinnati Poetry Review: "Railroad Yard in Rockhill Furnace."
Crab Orchard Review: "Sea Level Rising."
Flights: "Ghazal of the Arabian Nights."
The Gettysburg Review: "Language Lesson," "The Maid Train," "Music of the Spheres."
High Plains Literary Review: "Matinee."
Hotel Amerika: "Leap and Tumble."
The Hudson Review: "Great South Bay."
Inertia: "Contrary Motion."
The Journal: "Baptism," "Morning in Huntingdon, Pennsylvania."
The Literary Review: "The Cemetery Island" (first three sections).
Measure: "Sharing the Island" (part four of "The Cemetery Island").

Memphis State Review: "Consignment," "Thinking of Easter."

The New Republic: "Burning the Flags," "Retreat," "Sonnet to *Orpheus.*"

North American Review: "Falling in Love at the YMCA Pool."

The Paris Review: "The Palaces of Night."

Schuylkill Valley Journal of the Arts: "A Boy's Room," "Familiar World," "Gigi by the Zattere," "Meeting in Water."

Smartish Pace: "Christmas Tree Inn," "Circle Line."

Southern Indiana Review: "Natural History."

The Southern Review: "Heron."

Sou'wester: "Basic Training," "Glassy Apparatus," "Sonnets for Mr. Lewis."

Tampa Review: "Honeymoon in Venice."

Valparaiso Poetry Review: "In the Green Room with Robert Lowell."

Western Humanities Review: "Hareton Earnshaw, 1803: 'Hareton Earnshaw, 1500,'" "The Turkish Dishwasher."

Willow Springs: "Double Elegy."

The first three sections of "The Cemetery Island" were reprinted in *Burning the Aspern Papers* (Miami University Press, 2003).

Grants from the Charles Phelps Taft Foundation of the University of Cincinnati have given me free time in which to work on many of these poems. Gregory Dowling gave me crucial advice that helped me correct and expand "The Cemetery Island." I would like to thank Murray Bodo, Jim Cummins, Norma Jenckes, Pat Mora, Bea Opengart, and Peter Stitt for their generous help. I would also like to thank Alex Pepple for his attentive, helpful editing and his beautiful design of this book. I'm especially grateful to Richard Howard for accepting many of my poems for magazines he has edited, for his stimulating causeries that often spurred me to new drafts, and for his friendship, which I cherish. I owe more than thanks to LaWanda Walters—my wife, my muse, and my most faithful and demanding critic.

Contents

Acknowledgments — *vi*

I: *The Law that Nothing's Permanent but Change*

Girl on a Fishing Boat — *5*
Baptism — *6*
Sea Level Rising — *8*
Meeting in Water — *9*
Heron — *10*
Coastal Warning Displays — *11*
The Palaces of Night — *12*
Gigi by the Zattere — *14*
The Cemetery Island — *15*
Glassy Apparatus — *19*
Falling in Love at the YMCA Pool — *20*
Crossing the Lagoon — *21*
Honeymoon in Venice — *23*
Great South Bay — *26*
Circle Line — *27*

II: *By the Grace of Cross-Purposes*

Contrary Motion — *33*
Leap and Tumble — *34*
The Maid Train — *36*
Morning in Huntingdon, Pennsylvania — *38*
Retreat — *39*

Sonnet to *Orpheus*	*40*
Music of the Spheres	*41*
How to Stay Awake	*43*
Language Lesson	*45*
Hareton Earnshaw, 1803:	
"Hareton Earnshaw, 1500"	*46*
Ghazal of the Lutanist	*47*
To a Mockingbird	*48*
Christmas Tree Inn	*50*
A Boy's Room	*51*
Familiar World	*52*

III: *Already the Trees of Heaven Are Taking Over*

Sonnets for Mr. Lewis	*55*
In the Green Room with Robert Lowell	*60*
Basic Training	*61*
Double Elegy	*63*
Railroad Yard in Rockhill Furnace	*65*
Song with a Bridge	*67*
Ghazal of the Arabian Nights	*68*
The Turkish Dishwasher	*69*
Thinking of Easter	*70*
Burning the Flags	*71*
Consignment	*73*
Matinee	*74*
Right-of-Way	*75*
Natural History	*77*

Sea Level Rising

I
The Law that Nothing's Permanent but Change

Girl on a Fishing Boat

I loitered long enough beside Long Wharf,
watching the captains setting out their nets
and trotlines. One day, finally, it happened:
the skipper of a draketail looked my way,
grinned, his cracked face ablaze, inviting me
aboard to ride through sundown on the water.

It might have happened sooner for a boy,
the call to sea, the watermen relenting.
"Honey," he said, "Go starboard and let out
them traps." But he was not addressing me.
That's how they talked together, old salts cruising
for oysters, crabs, whatever was in season.

I sat out on the bow and felt the thrust
of wind, the rush of mist against my skin,
the seagulls jubilant, the ospreys calm
on nests they built on pilings, mallards flushed
to sudden flight in low trajectories
then rising, banking toward the flowing grass

of marshes that diminished as we sailed,
flat land disintegrating in the sea.
I reveled as the living figurehead
who brought good luck to sweet, tough watermen,
welcoming wind, clear sky, and endless water,
the elements crazing my unpainted face.

Baptism

A man in denim wades into the river
and turns, waist deep, in the polluted water.
Back on shore, men in dark suits and tall boys
in white robes amble to the grassy edge
of the narrow beach, while women, dressed in gowns
of aqua, scarlet, lemon, take their time
approaching the wide water. Then a boy
takes his first step in the Choptank River, guided
by two deacons. And the women start a hymn:
God is a good god.
                       Yes he is!
                                     I think
of swimming here, the jellyfish that stung me,
seaweed that scared me when it brushed my leg.
My son is piling stones on a picnic table,
here in the park that used to be a marsh.
"These are houses," he tells me. "It's our city."
It looks like a cemetery by the sea,
a jumble of tombstones, then a sheer drop.

The preacher holds the boy who's taller than he is
by the shoulders, roars a stream of holy words,
and gently dunks the boy, who flails back up
and hops to shore, repeating hallelujahs.
Hymns and thank-yous rise from the families.
My son keeps adding pebbles to his town,
metropolis of everyone he loves—
family, friends, house cats, heroes from cartoons.

Upstream, past tilting masts of the yacht club,
I see the hospital where I was born,
the same wide riverside where a tall boy
finds himself reborn as a springbok, bounding,
where a drenched preacher waits, where waves ease in,
and boys take off their soaked robes in sedans,
emerging in the dark pressed suits of men,
where vivid women chant, answering back
as constantly as waves that keep on landing
on shards of oyster shells, where my son charts
his future in a mass of piled-up stones
that all embody light and give off breath,
where something base is converted to a blessing:
song from shout, bare sky, pure dirty water.

Sea Level Rising

Water that threatens every place I love
is what I love about those lowland places
with rowboats moored to pilings in a cove
enclosed by loblolly pines, spartina grasses.

Inland, I sense it when I'm happiest,
a salt breeze blowing past the empty fields.
But nothing oceanic surges past
dark roads, the stubbly acres of dull golds.

I miss the rising tides that bash the docks
and spatter brackish water in my face,
reflections of bungalows and crab shacks
quaking in waves and almost breaking loose.

Sometimes, when fog wells up in the ravine
and overwhelms the valley's railroad tracks,
I feel at home, giddy until the sun
scatters the city's temporary lakes.

Then everything burns off. Sun glares. I miss
the fluent surface, the ever-shifting shore.
The shallowest lagoon would do! I'd bless
the moving waters, ripples everywhere.

Meeting in Water

She rose up from the nettle-netted bay,
grinning as if she knew me, her wet hair red.
Somehow the evangelist's summer day
led to dark water, bikinis, a casino,
and then a late night bus ride to get acquainted,
flirting in the forbidden lighter's glow,
touching, a secret zipper from arm to foot,
in the swimsuit-wet seat as the bus lurched.

Somehow religion mixed with sex. She attended,
for example, a Catholic school for girls, but landed,
after dancing to the Temptations, in my lap,
her dry hair blonde. Late at night, by a church,
a steeple stuck on top like a dunce cap,
we kissed and touched in the Presbyterian lot.

Heron

In Gray Marsh, on my way home, sunset smeared
above the trees, a great blue heron stepped
in shallow water, but when I appeared
by needlerushes near the path, he stopped.

The Choptank started boiling, white bursts over
the surface with its agitated light:
clustered eruptions, bubbling on the river
as catfish rose, lunging with appetite.

The heron, taking big slow steps, moved down
the riverbank, away from rollicking fish
you'd think would interest him as a real boon.
He waded, courting darkness, in no rush

to make his way, scouting for what could be
a trap, with no bait but tranquility.

Coastal Warning Displays

Red pennants hoisted up a flagpole bring
the bugeyes, sloops, and skipjacks in to port.
Pale undersides of leaves are clamoring
for mercy. Wind cups spin. Faint rumbles start.

From room to room, a woman yanks the plugs
from sockets, shuts the windows, turns the phone
receiver over in its cradle, lugs
her cat in from the stoop, goes out alone:

gold-haired old lady, lighting an Old Gold
on her screen porch, poised in a rocking chair
to watch the newsreels of the sky unfold.
The wind can't do much to her fringe of hair

but thrills her like the brass of an overture.
She rocks. The storm itself is calming her.

The Palaces of Night

1.

The beds are always made, and bright hallways
veer off like lanes, looking for canals to leap
across in a white arch, and the stairs rise
to other bedrooms, nothing but bedrooms, or drop
to further hallways, long rugs, lamps, the smell
of lilacs mingling with magnolia blossoms
though I don't see a flower vase at all—
merely a creamy sunlight in the rooms.

It makes me happy an ordinary house
could have bedchambers moor to it at night,
a floating hotel or cruise ship drifting loose
until the yard's an ocean, gardens of white
gardenias rising with the crests of waves
and vanishing again beneath the eaves.

2.

My house asleep—an archipelago
of airy rooms with moonlight in the mirrors—
opens its doors in welcome, as I go
discovering that what I thought were terrors
gladden and soothe: a comforter on each
iron bed, and transom lights above the doors,
doors that are louvered, as if near a beach
to catch the breezes and the sea's low slurs.

The palaces of night go on forever.
Each door I push, as if to step outside,
opens on rippling halls that zigzag, river
and tributaries, where I'm free to wade
between the quiet islands, reaching land
that shines, illuminated by sheer wind.

Gigi by the Zattere

A boat that carries water to cruise ships
rocks in her moorings by a café's dock.
Her mast's accompanied by faucets, pipes,
plumbing that runs along the raised green deck
above a scaly hull, water inside
and out, a packhorse for a salty planet.

A painter, on a bridge, is painting her,
wiping his brush on the stone rail to clean it.
He sketches the rough men who hop on board
and pull orange ropes off iron bollards. They're
backing up, rust-crusted propeller turning,
the pilot lighting up a cigarette.

Massive as palaces, the liners wait
down the long quay, white in the aqua morning.

The Cemetery Island

1. At Ezra Pound's Grave, 1994

Still rocking from the vaporetto ride
I wander,
         camera for amulet, past
blocks of stacked tombs:
         photographs behind glass
         and sconces of bouquets.

Lost in long alleys, I turn
         and stumble upon
cypresses in the walled plot
         for foreigners
    (who isn't in this true Serenissima?)
         overgrown with heaps
of broken statues, bashed slabs, crosses
                 in pieces.

At last
        (since my first trip to Venice in 1972)
                   I arrive:
        an ivy raft
with a tree for mast, a hatch of carved marble.

I snap a laurel leaf from the green crown
and press it in a currency receipt,
        wipe dirt from the name

        (and what admirer does otherwise?)
                the slab
flattened to the earth's curve,
                        trap door
                            sealed to the underworld.

2. What Thou Lovest Well, 1997

Now that Olga Rudge has moved in, the plot's arranged in a family portrait: two tilted slabs, like name plates on an office desk, framed in a white border with a half-moon extension in front, geometrically Palladian. A carved urn with a dead plant sits in the semi-circle. Sawed-off stumps poke out near the rear line segment, the earth cracked from all the beautiful days in the treacherous lagoon.

3. At Joseph Brodsky's Grave, 1997

There's a white cross, with pebbles on the arms
and peak, more offerings heaped up below—
a vase of daisies, a blue can with terms
in Hebrew lettering, a candle's glow
inside (and in a red translucent jar
with a gold lid)—for this last seminar.

How did he manage to be buried here,
the lucky stiff? Unsanctioned by the chaplain,
apart from where the other Russians are,

Jewish by birth, not Ezra's fan, light rippling
through cypresses, the push of the lagoon
against pocked Istrian marble, a surge of brine.

So now the island has a grove of bards,
a college of silence, where the shade refreshes
and lizards skitter under hidden birds.
A vaporetto's diesel motor hushes
when it maneuvers past the crumbling walls,
and sparrows comment with their quietest calls.

4. Sharing the Island, 2013

> The Cantos, *too, left me cold; the main error was an old one: questing after beauty. For someone with such a long record of residence in Italy, it was odd that he hadn't realized that beauty can't be targeted, that it is always a by-product of other, often very ordinary pursuits.*
> —*Joseph Brodsky,* Watermark

The cross was temporary, but the stone—
his engraved name in Roman and Cyrillic—
is temporary, too, in the long run.
Arched at the top, appropriately phallic,
the marker has its offerings of pens,
as though the poet might keep on composing
paeans and laments to the lagoon's
thin film of beauty, tides that keep on rising.

Pound might not like him either, but they're stuck,
no exit as their voices boom and volley—
how odd that their delivery sounds alike—
although to passersby in the quiet alley

between their resting places, only wind
and warbler moan, a forecast for the drowned.

Glassy Apparatus

I'm drunk in a distillery of light
that makes me woozy, rocking on canals
past rosy and eroding bricks, past walls
of gothic windows, past a glittery fleet.

Here, everything's in flux, repeated spasms
of wake and wave, bright sun, reflecting pool,
surges made up of intricate detail.
From window boxes, flowers hang like prisms.

Light flutters on the undersides of bridges,
spattering on the basin's sizzling grill,
bursting like gunfire, drizzled like swirls of oil,
flashing against the *polizia*'s badges.

Sun spent, the water shows off what it's got:
a sheet of gold leaf, crumpled, then pressed flat.

Falling in Love at the YMCA Pool

Water's a quick conductor, the way a storm
    seeks out a bather swimming laps
        and strikes like Zeus. A surge

electric in its force connects from me
    to you, twin shocks in this blue pool.
        Our toes can feel the cracks

along the slanting, nubby, concrete bottom
    as kids splash by, jeering at friends
        who can't jog through packed liquid.

Crisscrossed ripples, rumpled as bed sheets, push
    below your breasts, wetting the cups,
        and lap on my chest hairs.

We talk of ordinary things and look
    straight in each other's eyes, yours gray,
        mine hazel, standing an arm's

length apart, feeling the wind rise, the water
    touching us everywhere, all over
        in a slow dance's groove.

Crossing the Lagoon

The boat was packed. The others in my group
had jostled for some benches in the cabin,
but I stood at the railing, brushing against
a large man in a charcoal suit, a mother
fussing to keep two children by her side.
The sun was up, silvering the wave crests,
and land was distant, twisted strips of green,
except for islands, now and then, brick ruins
and cranes with piles of building materials.
Wide water. And then, from way back when, "The water
is wide." The motor of the water-bus
rumbled so numbly, I began to sing
in murmurs, "I cannot get over," thinking
of you, my love, across the ocean's time zones,
as two old men stood in a *sandolo*
and rowed the other way, "and neither have
I wings to fly," as gulls accompanied
our groaning boat and sunlight mixed with breezes,
a tangible brocade of hot and cold.
"Give me a boat," I hummed, "that can carry two,"
and wanted you here, cramped beside the railing,
where we could not help touching, flank to flank.
Our hands would have to clasp. We'd sing together,
unheard by others, while the engine throbbed.
"And we'll both row," we'd swear, "my love and I."
How could we cross the distances between us?
The mate, emerging from the pilot house,

parted the crowd by muttering *"Permesso."*
His tossed rope curled around the metal post
and made the boat glide in against the dock
that floated, bumping the pier. How could I cross
the dark lagoon that opened into ocean,
rowing against the waves that rose and rose?

Honeymoon in Venice

A bottle of prosecco greeted us
in La Calcina, our front room with a view
of the wide canal, the island of Giudecca.
John Ruskin's room was right next door to ours,
but we fared better on our honeymoon.
His pheromones were triggered by the Gothic
arches and foils, not hard-core fleshiness
of a real woman with real body hair,
his wedding surprise. Our own carnality
got us in trouble we could not resist,
a pair of long-time friends and fellow artists
who plunged into romantic complications,
years of my dithering, a legal slough
we likened to the slow process in *Bleak House.*

But when we made love, that first afternoon,
feeling a sea breeze, hearing the boats and waves,
each other's odalisque, we were incensed
that baggage handlers or airport security
inspected our vibrator so hard it broke.
It hummed like a power drill but didn't shimmy.
It figured, since our love affair and friendship
had always been tempestuous, not calm.

She needed medicine, so I took a walk,
looking for the nearest *farmacia,*
but the shop at San Trovaso wasn't open.

I kept on looking for green neon crosses,
stopping on bridges, gazing at canals
where someone sloshed a mop on a boat's deck
and workers hoisted paving stones from barges.

Near Byron's palace on the Grand Canal,
blue screens kept off the cruising paparazzi
who trolled in boats, lusting for a shot
of Angelina Jolie. But my LaWanda
raged at the arrogance of stardom, swore
she'd never see *The Tourist,* in production
while we were honeymooning in the city.
I said I'd never *pay* to see the movie,
but still, it was a record of our stay,
and if we could ignore the silly thriller
it might become a kind of photo album:
sunny nostalgia, tinged with a bitter edge.

Scornful of cars, I didn't want to sully
our honeymoon by going to the Lido,
but she insisted we couldn't miss the beach,
sorry it wasn't warm enough to swim.
We took a bus—after the water-bus—
and got off at the Grand Hôtel des Bains,
closed for the season, despite the ghosts of Mann
and Aschenbach. We walked past the cabanas
and men who were playing soccer on the beach,
so she could wade in the Adriatic Sea.
I knew how wrong I'd been to discourage her

from joy that made her radiant as the wave tips
dizzy with sunlight, cresting with tidal surges.
Love wasn't rigid but resilient,
open to change, eager to divorce
anything impeding its energy.

The whole time we were there, she wouldn't visit
a single church, despite the Tintorettos,
but wouldn't miss the shrine of Harry's Bar,
savoring martinis, popping olives
in our mouths. The high point of the trip
came when the suave proprietor, named for the bar,
approached from behind, holding her chair to help
her from the table—Arrigo Cipriani
smiling and flirting with my vibrant bride.

Great South Bay

Driving at midnight, depressed,
heading nowhere in particular
over whistling tracks, past wide porches,
looking for a landmark or the way back,
suddenly it blackened:
water, the bay, an island
of dock lights blinking on the rim.

I coasted down the pier.
A car flashed its headlights, answered
by moving specks. Huddled men,
orange from a lantern,
baited their hooks from a darkened bucket.
A dinghy, poled in shallows,
trawled for killies with a handheld net.

Yet everything was hushed:
a distant horn, a fisherman
loading rods and tackle in a boat
on the pier-high waves,
the whole pier muffled to whispers
in the clearing of night,
in the water's wide basilica.

Circle Line

1.

Around the city in a crooked loop,
a lasso ready to jerk tight, we ride
the double-decker boat, while seagulls swoop
and soar, then turn, returning in a glide
and trailing us from harbor to Hell's Gate.
Whether I'm with my father or my son,
we don't talk much on the slick deck. We wait
at the stern railing for the other one
to summon up the words and swing around
the rocky puzzlement that's like this place:
jagged, dirty, huge, with a raucous sound
of rumbling, horns, and motors, a ground bass
of song, like one I learned when, clearing his throat,
my father taught me "Row, Row, Row Your Boat."

2.

My father taught me "Row, Row, Row Your Boat"
was called a *round*. The singers entered in
at different bars but stopped on the same note
parted by time. So all these rides begin,
"The deck's an ashtray," the announcer laughs.
We pass by glass facades, columned and lined
like newspapers whose front-page photographs
are plywood sheets where windows lost to wind.
We pass a tilting, fifty-foot coffee cup,
the Assay Office where silver lines the smokestack,

floating under bridges, looking up
at shadows where a gull dips low, then strokes back.
And each ride's different, but the same, as we're
departing from an isolated pier.

3.

Departing from an isolated pier,
we might as well have boarded the book I used
for a tour boat when playing on the floor,
trips to my father's one-room flat. I cruised
around the braided rug where I had placed
a statue of the Empire State Building.
On warped linoleum, my vessel raced.
He'd planned to be a singer, so he'd sing
"Toyland" while I played, sad that he'd left
a place where he could not fit in again.
He meant his warbling tenor as a gift,
more than the souvenir of where we'd been,
floating around the island, where we found
we were spinning on a dizzying merry-go-round.

4.

We were spinning. On a dizzying merry-go-round,
we heard that a football team could line the hands
of a clock we passed. For my son and me, it's rained
for the whole trip, but neither of us stands
or leaves the open deck. We share a bench,
willing enough to get our bottoms wet.
As usual, we don't say much. Rains drench

our pants and jackets, but we're not upset.
The passing view's enough, an opening,
allowing for silence that is not a gap
but love, as much as any words we sing.
We're sharing what we can, rocked by the slap
of wake from a Coast Guard cutter, enjoying
the route, as regular as a wedding ring.

5.

The route, as regular as a wedding ring,
runs counterclockwise, as it really should—
like plates that rode on flatcars, clattering
along the counter near Times Square, the food
arriving with a toot in the Hamburger Train.
Long gone, of course, the locomotive's tracks
that tunneled to the kitchen and back again.
The past's a code that no one really cracks.
When Poe was working as an editor
near City Hall, he liked to take a swim
across the river to the Brooklyn shore
and back again, the currents fighting him.
Now no one's in the water. And it's strange,
the law that nothing's permanent but change.

6.

The law that nothing's permanent but change
makes music matter. Before my son could say
a word, he hummed and pattered out a range
of music to accompany his play.

Now, after silence, he habitually
resorts to clicks and humming for his thoughts.
He paces on the playground. Teachers agree
it seems unhealthy, the solo way he floats
around the school. But I don't think it's wrong
to improvise on solitude like that.
It's in our blood. And when we hear a song,
we add our descants and collaborate
with counter-melodies, a trait that says
all three of us have sung in choruses.

7.

All three of us have sung in choruses
and live for music, one way or another,
my father's oratorios, the jazz
my son is learning to improvise. We gather
together through affinities of song,
my son's circle of fifths, my father's rounds.
It doesn't mean that we don't get along
if we're not talkative, for all these sounds
unite us like a triad. I listen while
my son is playing scales. In a photograph
we stand behind a lifesaver and smile
before embarking, anxious to cast off,
thrilled as reporters looking for a scoop
around the city in a crooked loop.

II

By the Grace of Cross-Purposes

Contrary Motion

        In Harmony class,
analyzing Bach, we graphed how the sopranos,
           descending, were countered
    by the basses' upward rise,
like friends converging at a pool hall halfway up
    or down a city hillside.
I thought of fireworks, spattering like water bombs,
dripping past the rockets launched from an island,
        each new gusher displayed in a black lake.

        Later, in Chorus,
I painted staves between strips of masking tape,
           silent as vocal parts
    caromed against each other.
I learned to sing by shutting up. I learned how
    lines take shape beneath the smear
of white latex, the tangling of choristers.
Ripping the ribbons off the board, I almost laughed
     at the drips, hanging like socks from taut lines.

I liked being quiet as the choir soared, following
the collision course of notes. I even liked
    the paint leaked away from the clean
    horizontal lines. And now, I want
both sides of any squabble, pros and cons,
to rise by the grace of cross-purposes—
       like a crumpled roof
        retimbered, beams abutting,
reaching their pitch through opposition.

Leap and Tumble

   What's more athletic
  than the mind—poised like a forward
  limbering at the free-throw line,
cocking his arm and shoving it toward the basket, then
  stopping, steadying, and with a flick
  of his fingertips, lofting the ball
   in a high, extravagant arc,
a ferris wheel's curve, as it shoots
   and rushes to the net,
  floating through the interwoven ropes.

   One point. But in the mind,
  his shot's already the moving
  loom of a fountain in Munich,
water curling at the lip then dropping, in single
  bursts of liquid you can follow down.
  It's the wind, suddenly gone, silver leaves
   upturned like the throats of children,
like Isaac, a stillness teetering
   as the blades of dark rain
  gather and thresh across the fairways.

  What rises and returns
approaches music, a blessing
beyond sound, the way the orchestra
pauses in the overture of *The Magic Flute,*
  just after commotion, and then the strings

       resume, pianissimo.
It's like waiting for a lover who's underwater—
       or a loon coming up
    at different spots in Walden Pond—
or the prowess of a capsule, curving home
       to a perfect splashdown,
    or the rope bridge over rapids
into which you drop your fist of bills.

The Maid Train

Throughout the night
I wake up to check the clock,
clutching it like a grenade, hoping for time
before the alarm at five.

One day, the knob has vanished
from the door downstairs. I hurry
back up, squeezing myself through a window
and down the fire escape, dropping the metal ladder.

One day, the hall is white with smoke,
but damp, a steam cock left open.
I inch through the indoor cloud,
my sweater drenched, my glasses useless.

Expecting to be scalded, I step into clarity.
Looking back up, I'm surprised
by the crowds in windows, smiling and waving.
One woman even claps.

On the early train, commuting
to the suburbs away from rush-hour traffic,
I drift outdoors to the covered swimming pools
and the still-dark windows.

The train's half full of cleaning women.
I want to say they look sad,
footsore, but just as I knot silk ties
under laundry-shrunken collars,

they're stylish in heels or deck shoes,
plumed with bright scarves,
frosted coiffures, almost elegant
in tinted designer glasses.

When we reach our station,
they glide down the platform,
cargoed with Florentine handbags.
One of them totes a briefcase.

As the train lights glint on the tracks,
we slip by the warning gate
and cross to a chorus line of taxis.
The train sweeps off with a Bronx cheer.

Morning in Huntingdon, Pennsylvania

I'm wearing a toupee of clouds
by the bean field, the orderly rows
like soldiers in green camouflage
crawling their way to the far woods
behind the security fence of trees.
The railroad's prospering—long freights
tolling the crossing gate's bells
several times an hour. The railroad's
prospering; but so's the river,
the Juniata, where kayakers
are paddling in shadows near the bank.
Welders are working on the main line,
their torches sparking as the sun
lights up the rails. The Amtrak train
is late, two hours late, from Pittsburgh,
and a friendly, white-haired woman
(the station agent?) in the shack that serves
as ticket booth and waiting room
doesn't know why. It's a good day
to be late, pull off on the shoulder
of U.S. 22 and take notes
for my life list. The only hairpiece
I'll endorse is shade from the changeable sky.

Retreat

Amazing that the shrapnel of the light
tousles the ferns and the wild phlox. Amazing
how fields give way to woods, oak groves, how flat
pastureland explodes in ravines—then, rising
to crests and ridges where glaciers once scooped
Ohio's malleable terrain, reverses
itself: the violence of the land still kept
yet, amazingly, kept still. What surprises
must be in all things! Dragonflies, for instance,
or windows whose crazed panes flow gradually,
transforming the transparency of gin
on an oak credenza. What would I be
without these shattering views? A creek's pistons,
the off-white fireworks of the dandelion!

Sonnet to *Orpheus*

> *Tell Jean Cocteau I love him—the only one who plunges into the myth which lies open to him and from which he returns tanned as from the seashore.*
> —Rilke

O tree in the waves! O auricle in the tree!
The radio waves break foaming on the shore
of my apartment. Muse, do you hear me?
A grove within the dark zone of a mirror
gives passage to the underworld, a passage
of string quartet, thorny with accidentals.
Branches erupt in static there. *Sois sage:*
even the noise, with time, becomes contrapuntal.

With time. A tree. A passage. Where can the spiral
coil but inward, music whirled to the endless
pinwheel of galaxies? The tree becomes choral,
the waves hyperbolic, and the grove windless.

The animals, with time, convene in sessions
to monitor the crystal's faint transmissions.

Music of the Spheres

Every alien, the kind from outer space,
    is terrible
at showing up at any reasonable place

    like Central Park
or the nearest municipal court. Habeas corpus
    doesn't work

when there's no body, no protoplasm, to have.
    But let's assume
they're out there, however far away they live,

    distant as angels
who flirt and play hard to get, eluding
    our radar vigils,

keeping us under surveillance, learning to feign
    our own good looks,
hide slimy tentacles, brilliantly mundane

    or colorful as comics.
Why will we never know a close encounter?
    Economics.

Except in the solar systems of theory, what planet
    would be exempt
from budget crises? The mystery of this whodunit

    makes a bad plot.
No one will ever break through. Not us. Not them.
    There's no Starfleet

but what we conjure up, the fantasy
    of making contact
with what we can't know, the nothing we still see.

How to Stay Awake

Late at night on the interstate, driving
    while drowsy, you crank
open the window so the wind starts shoving

    with its cold fingers.
But even with coffee, the sedative is silence,
    a calm that lingers

in the slow drone of tires on the highway,
    like the hushed waves
against a hull that's rocking on the bay.

    In any car,
the wind, however loud, is still a murmur.
    What's a sure

way to keep yourself awake? Just click
    the radio on
to something loud enough, not talk but rock,

and don't just listen—
    that's how a siren lures you to slip under,
seductive assassin,

and merge into a gulf of harmonies.
    You have to sing,
open your mouth wide, belt it out, and praise

      the means you have
for rescuing your own self from yourself,
      to stay alive

by keeping the muscles moving in your mouth,
      so your eyes can't close,
so the song becomes a counterspell to death.

Language Lesson

Rigor and *consequences*
vie for the title of "World's Ugliest Word,"
    bullying the senses

that take their daily vacations in the hammock
    of late afternoon.
Life's hard enough without a poke in the stomach

    meaning "reduce"
or "sit up straight" or "see?" or "now you've done it."
    Done what? Been loose

instead of tight, or tight in the sense of drunk,
    Li Bai drowning
in moonlight on the river? Who wouldn't shrink

    from pettiness,
the rule of rules, dictatorship of the mean
    and merciless?

Grasshoppers, Joyce's "grace hopers," dance
    a quickening reel
instead of plodding to the same death that ants

    cannot forestall.
Go out rigid? Pleading guilty? No, go out
    joyous, full.

Hareton Earnshaw, 1803:
"Hareton Earnshaw, 1500"

Before I spelled the letters of my name
    the world was rocky outcrops, hidden drops
into old quarries, firs the winds overcame
    with their harassment, the grounded treetops.

Above the door, carved letters. When I entered
    the shadowy room, with dogs in every nook,
I grunted and I swore. My world was centered
    on fire and sleep. Then I unwrapped the book

she placed upon my knees, and opened it,
    and something sprang open in me—like wine
searing me to life. When my eyes lit
    on the bright page, it spelled out "Catherine."

Ghazal of the Lutanist

Ever Dowland, ever doleful, the lutanist says come again
to melancholy, whether he's silent or plays "Come Again."

Invitations that mention "deadly pain" and wail "out, alas"
won't seduce anyone but a masochist who prays *Come! Again!*

Torches at court leave shadows for uneasy liaisons,
dark rooms where ladies-in-waiting, in silent lays, come again.

Courtiers whisper on back stairs, place notes in ruffled sleeves,
but the lutanist can't catch the phrase. Come again?

The page rubs his eyes before stretching gut strings along the lute
and poking around for the tuning peg's eye. Dark days come again.

When panes of leaded glass fill like goblets with tinted light,
John is fingering scales on his lute as sun rays come again.

To a Mockingbird

    You there, on the light pole,
crooning and trilling an early wake-up call,
twitching your long tail, beating time in dress gray,
I'm glad you're back, though you've always meant trouble.
    In boot camp, you heckled me
at the firing range. I wanted to blast you.
But then the harshness modulated
into water music, airs, fire sirens—
"Heads up!" I heard, and squeezed the trigger
    before the order to fire.

    Now and then, you pop in
and pop off, yodeling, meowing, rejecting
nothing as beneath your mimicry. You come back
like my flying dreams—a reservoir below me
    as I push the plush air lower,
drifting in a hum that never resolves
to a final chordal thump, but runs on and on
like your whatever-happens melody.
Pillager of neighborhoods, broadcasting
    your loot, melted down to loose tunes.

You make it look easy, arranging
charm bracelets of hammerings, gate creaks,
alarm clocks, and whistling teakettles—
    inviting in everything.
Try sticking around. We'll bang a dusty broom

on the railing. Take a pinch
of that clang, and the next sounds that buzz.
Hit me with your razzmatazz.

Christmas Tree Inn

My parents came here a week after D-Day,
an officer on furlough with his bride,
honeymooning by a Maine lake. I drive
past evergreens, following faded signs
of Christmas trees to the sprawling red house
with docks and tennis courts, weeds breaking through
the baseline. A woman dressed in a bikini
answers my knock. It's private now, she says,
but here's a postcard, come along for the tour.

I see where the guests gathered in the evening,
a porch above the lake, a grand piano,
and nod. I see where they met for cordials,
the great stone hearth, a balcony rising.
I look hard at the honeymoon post, gouged
with initials and plus signs, but can't make out
their marks. In the bedrooms, white coverlets
are studded with embroidered Christmas trees.

The blue of the lake is so deep, unearthly—
no wonder they came here, seeking relief
in a world apart. I can't understand
how beauty like this fails to sustain us.

When my own marriage ended, the last thing
we bought was a tree, a brittle pine,
one side flattened on the supermarket lot.
We trimmed it with woven angels and lit it:
a hearth fire kindled with the wrappings of gifts.

A Boy's Room

With tiny wads of Play-Doh, he has fashioned
scorpions, Io moths, red velvet mites,
water spiders emerging from thick air sacs,
Japanese beetles perched upon white petals.
He places them in his secret gallery—
a Danish Modern liquor cabinet—
to let them dry. He loves assassin bugs
and Congo chafers. He listens for the sound
of hissing cockroaches and tinfoil beetles
clicking against their luminous green shells.

He hates the words "explode" and "blow" and "burst."
He knows we have a nest of paper wasps
in the kitchen's ventilator. He knows
we find it odd that people find it odd.
He knows that when we quarrel, the house walls hum
like glassed-in hives of honey bees at the zoo.
He hopes and fears that when the wings beat loudest,
the house will lift above the tall catalpas
and he'll look down at miniature explosions:
fireflies rising from a darkened crater.

Familiar World

"Autistic Teen Found Missing," a bulletin announces, reporting
    how a boy left the clinic,
his mother pleading, search parties in the woods, a doctor
    explaining the process of auditory therapy:
a patient listens through headphones to hours of soothing music
    (but never any words),
until he can tolerate the noises of an average day.

Everyone expects the obvious, but two clerks at a Redi-Mart
    notice a boy behind their store.
He had followed a creek, sleeping under bushes in a lair where
    mosquitoes spotted him,
covered him in welts, and when he finally climbed up the slippery
    bank, the highway was strange,
a different glare of neon and headlights.

In some tales, the boy would keep on following the creek beyond
    rapids, across a ford,
until he came to a pool where light collected and something rose
    to the misty surface,
promising to grant his wishes: how to talk, how to bear the noises,
    how to find
a familiar world within the foreign.

III

Already the Trees of Heaven Are Taking Over

Sonnets for Mr. Lewis

1.

Hunting for people on the Internet,
I stumbled on my English teacher's name
from junior high: "openly gay . . . Corvette-
driving . . . died from a heart attack . . . ." It came

as news to me, who cowered through ninth grade
and owe him everything, learning the words
of poems he cut out, mounted, and displayed:
Eliot, Hopkins, Yeats on bulletin boards.

Authority, though, was jolting, like a slap
of water on a schooner, when the bay
rose and struck back at faulty seamanship.
How can I thank him now? How can I say

I'll always be your student, and you'll be
the hidden voice that keeps on prodding me?

2.

He roared "I can't stand chaos!" with the glare
of a literary führer at a rally,
pacing, his fingers brushing a shock of hair
from his forehead, menacing as a bully.

Never had any lessons been so hushed
as when his "good class" cringed, the unhappy few
who waited on that shore where breakers crashed.
Walking down Massachusetts Avenue,

under a railroad bridge, up a long hill
of log steps, past Little Falls Library
to junior high, its locker-jostled halls,
I dawdled under the maples' canopy.

Though a bad pupil, shirking homework, still
I hovered in his classroom after school.

3.

My classmates who were friends (or so I assume)
picked up the briefcase from beside my chair
and passed it to the far side of the room.
After the bell, they launched it down the stairs.

And they were right to rid me of the prop,
my stab at better learning through office supplies.
Sitting there, quiet, listening, I dropped
the pseudo-intellectual disguise.

For he expected us to start our novels,
compose a group of sonnets, diagram
the sentences of Proust, track articles
on index cards—his own curriculum.

I wanted a how-to guide, a nod that yes,
you're welcome in this world of consciousness.

4.

Someone must still be driving his Corvette
faster than any limits, itching to pass
the slowpokes through the mountains. He could get
inflamed by sluggishness! One day in class,

the anger he could usually restrain
broke like an open boat upon the strand.
He smashed his right fist through the windowpane
but came back, scrawling with his bandaged hand.

A fiery sports car for a fiery mind
reflected him. I didn't want to be
one of the "stones" that he could hardly stand
to have in class. And though I didn't hurry
doing much of anything, I did worry
his anger was about to fall on me.

5.

The trainer flicks her clicker, and the cat
leaps on the upright log and hurries up
to snatch a food reward. The ocelot,
easy with the long leash, pauses on top

until another click, then climbs back down,
headfirst, hugging the bark of the scarred tree,
tumbling onto a platform, stone on stone,
slinking its way back to captivity.

"We don't teach any tricks," the trainer says.
"They learn behaviors." But aren't the tricks what
everyone wants to learn, how to amaze
the public like a crafty acrobat?

"It matters, look, it matters," he insisted,
snapping his fingers at every moment wasted.

6.

Taking the curves
around jutting cliffs
and redwood bluffs,
the Stingray swerves
above ocean waves.
He downshifts, laughs
at the critics' gaffes
about recitatives
on the opera quiz.
The Pacific roars,
its bravos his
and the blazing car's.
Everything is
in the stars, in the stars.

7.

Like John Keats, peppering his tongue to feel
the soothing coolness of claret, he exposes
his flesh to the sun's mimicry of hell,
until he dives into the sea and rises
beyond the breakers, floating on a swell
and sinking in a trough. The salty breezes
can't blow him very far off shore. The pull
of tides can't hold him long, unless he chooses.

Today, he has the freedom of the beach,
no students haunting him. (He does the haunting,
for surely he must know that when you teach,
the lessons have the power of enchanting
for a lifetime of lost time.) Let him stand,
naked, exultant on the burning sand.

In the Green Room with Robert Lowell

I hate getting to the spot, making talk in the Green Room, going on.
—*from an interview*

I sat alone with him before the reading:
shy, awed by this big man who opened up
a black spring binder, probably the draft
of *Day by Day,* and marked and cut and scratched
with a red ballpoint pen on typed-up sheets.
My teacher had appointed me to guard him,
just in case he had a mental breakdown
and tried to wander off. But he kept writing,
or rewriting, on pages that looked bloody
with crossing out and cramped, inserted words.
I didn't say a thing, but kept on watching.
So I was startled, sitting at a distance,
when suddenly he looked up, smiled, and said,
"That's a nice green corduroy jacket."

Basic Training

Herbert Eugene Mulkey Jr Pfc Ar
5 Jun 52   Mt Airy MD
2 Mar 71   4W 17

After we swore the oath together, someone in the day room
    passed out Bibles. I refused mine.
Mulkey couldn't believe it. "Hey, man, you crazy? It's free.
    I'll take it."

He bunked beside me for the next few days. Once, he said, he
    went to school
late enough so the halls were empty, on the lookout for
    Musselman,
a white guy who swore he'd kick his ass when they ran into
    each other.
Cornered in the boys' room, Mulkey pulled out his mama's
    pistol
and grazed the bully in the arm, the bullet ricocheting over tiles
    and fixtures.

Halfway through basic training, running laps, I jammed my
    ankle
twice on the cinder track. It wasn't bad, just a sprain, but I used
    it for an excuse.
Flourishing my medical profile, swinging my way on crutches
    to the post library,
I didn't throw grenades, or go on bivouac, or wake up gasping
    through tear gas.

But how, when I got the order, could I avoid standing guard at
 the arsenal,
armed with live ammo, pacing after midnight in the rain that
 was heading our way?
When I showed up, Mulkey was there in his helmet and poncho
 and said, "Go on back now."
He took my guard duty, stood at attention in my place, stayed
 up as I slept.

That night he did me a favor strikes me as a hinge. A door
 opened
and I passed through, exaggerating a limp. His life, though, was
 already fixed—
earth tugging his boots, an unseen burst ripping through
 camouflage fatigues.

Now, when I think of his name gouged on a sunken wall, almost
 lost
among thousands, it's etched on my own face in the shining
 black mirror.

Double Elegy

—for Elizabeth Kray and Vladimir Ussachevsky

When I needed a jacket,
    Betty, you shepherded me
        upstairs to a secondhand
    shop on Third Avenue, found me
half of a herringbone suit,
    so light in summer I still
        wear it though it's unraveling.
    When I got married, you wrote
"I think it's a marvelous
    idea" and switched to two
        different pens as the ink failed.

When I had to find a room,
    you sublet your apartment
        on Claremont. e e cummings
    had painted on shirt cardboard
a landscape with a lone tree.
    I loved the grand piano,
        Vladimir's, and the tape spools
    everywhere. I loved walking
through the huge rooms in the dark,
    the slant of streetlamps, the moons
        of blue china on a ledge.

I thanked you, of course, but speech
    interfered with gratitude.
I learned this blessing only
    in retrospect. Now I prize
your story of Vladimir
    crossing the country by bus,
his upright disassembled
    and stowed in the cargo bay.
I find myself uttering
    "I see" and making your face,
retracing our walking tours
    near city hall, pointing out
the newspaper offices
    no longer there, the buildings
replaced by other buildings
    as we gazed at what remained:
a resonant emptiness,
    the mind's archaeology
of invisible layers,
    city on top of city.

Railroad Yard in Rockhill Furnace

It's like Pompeii,
but rather than ash, the pyroclastic flow,
the great eruption
struck when the bottom dropped out of the coal market.
Silver smokestacks
rise like nightmare cannon from the shops,
red and shabby,
idle as if a strike had shut them down.

Inside the walls
black with coal dust, under a shaky roof
sagging from snowfalls,
a stationary engine hunkers down,
connected to shafts
and leather belts that powered all the machines,
made steam enough
for car barn, foundry, blacksmith shop, sand tower.

A calendar
says 1956 inside the building,
the foreman's notes
spread out where he left them on a work bench,
ratchets and wrenches
hung where mechanics left them when they left
and padlocked the doors,
walking home through dusk, along the tracks.

It doesn't look
as though catastrophe had gutted out
the valley's length,
where all the excursion trains arrive on time
and boarded shops
still hold their power, like clocks that just need winding.
Although it all
remains intact, the physical plant's machines

and wood and steel,
nothing is still productive here, except
what always was:
blackberries by the roadbed, wildflowers
between cracked ties,
and all around the basin of the yard
the deep green peaks
subsiding gradually like ocean swells.

Song with a Bridge

The clouds are like a long, slow freight—
    they rumble, and their hoppers rain.
A crossing gate
    detains us for the endless train
        of wakefulness
        and worries that we're futureless.
It's getting late, it's getting late.

The always running candidate
    has talking points he can't explain
in the debate
    that's always rumbling in his brain.
        He won't confess
        in public that it's all a mess
and getting late, it's getting late.

And up ahead,
    beyond the cuts and fills,
        the dynamited trestle cracks
while we're in bed.
    A boy in denim spills
        his beer while following the tracks.

It's better, still, than the long wait
    for visions through a windowpane
while you work late,
    biding the hours that remain.
        Who wouldn't guess
        that in the middle of distress
it's getting late, it's getting late?

Ghazal of the Arabian Nights

I'm thinking of you, Abbas, my friend from long ago, away
from both our homes. Outside, my neighbor shovels snow away.

We tramped through drifts in Grenoble, en route to the *cinémathèque*.
The constant falling of dusty flakes made the alps go away.

My next-door neighbor in a gray suite of rooms, you played
folk music and teased my girlfriend, who sneaked in like a stowaway.

We didn't keep in touch, Abbas, but now my country's succeeded
in occupying yours, in putting a so-called foe away.

Maybe you're still in France, but I picture you on the streets
of Baghdad. I've tried to find you online, but I don't know a way.

It amazed me, studying abroad, our suite a miniature
United Nations, an Iranian student not a stone's throw away.

But a greenish light on domes and apartment blocks from the latest
campaign of bombs and missiles took my hopeful bravado away.

Where was Scheherazade when we needed her stories to enchant
inspectors who searched through palaces, to spirit the status quo away?

Listening to stories, the madcap mishaps of ordinary people,
inclines us towards love, immerses us, makes hardness flow away.

Abbas, this is John. I want the news to tell me you're alive.
May our grandest plans, like crumpled headlines, blow away.

The Turkish Dishwasher

crushes his cigarette on a counter
and goes out back, the screen door
whining, then slamming behind him.
On Long Island, near the end of winter,
a new beginning seems as distant
as a puma in a gulley, asleep, the tip
of his tail rising, white and yellow hairs
fluttering in the breeze.

Barbed wire twists
around the dogwood, an X
carved in its scaly bark.
When will buds blossom?
When will the chicken coop,
leaning against a maple, topple
into the gravelly yard?
He leans on the tilting wall,
not giving a push
but not propping it up either.

Istanbul is as far away
as Byzantium. He taps out
a cigarette from the floppy pack
and searches his pockets
for a match, the cigarette
fidgeting up and down his lips.

Thinking of Easter

At night, without my glasses, I see a cross,
foreshortened against the decaying, grave-gray sky.
It's really a telephone pole, though I can't
make out the wires, and it stands above a jumble
of concrete, broomstraws, and a broken staff,
a shovel blade blazing on the heap's crown.

At Easter, in Carmel, a priest intoned
"He is risen," but no one rose from their pews;
he had to clear his throat and repeat himself.
"Why do you seek the living among the dead?"
he uttered, just before a splurge of bells.
I took communion in my sneakers, sand from the beach
bunching at the toes. Later that day,
on the beach a few miles south, I stumbled upon
a sea lion, tattered and brittle in the sun.

The dead are our redemption—sharpening
the tang of cider, extrapolating a sunburst
on palmettos, shaking eucalyptus trees
that huddle, shaggy as buffaloes, on a ridge.
But even they can't resurrect the pine
of a telephone pole, blurry at midnight,
though it carries voices—even beyond themselves—
to what must surely be another world.

Burning the Flags

A one-armed boy crouches in gutter mud,
scooping an ochre lump with a tin can
on the hot street, where nothing but exhaust
rises in the faint wind, where nothing flies.

> *They're burning the flag of the Serengeti*
> *They're burning the flag of the Amazon*

The honor guard gets lost in the mausoleum,
letting out yelps at glass cases of bones,
gems in eye sockets. During a funeral,
they tangle the flag above a sergeant's coffin.

> *They're burning the flag of the Parthenon*
> *They're burning the banner of the Himalayas*

The toy standard-bearer of the Union
hoists a blue plastic tab upon a bridge
of papier-mâché, a plume of cotton bursting
from a lead cannon toward ranks of figurines.

> *They're burning the streamers of the Black Forest*
> *They're burning the colors of the Dead Sea*

The boy socks a Clorox bottle tethered
to a street sign, while his empty sleeve flaps.
Downhill, a decal's peeling on the cracked
windshield of a truck, stripes bleached out, stars clear.

They're burning the guidon of the Great Barrier Reef
They're burning the ensign of the Everglades
They're burning the fabric, they're burning the flags
of forest, oxygen, breath, and flags

Consignment

So much of what we most love comes to nothing:
sunlight flaring in a winter greenhouse;
a screened porch in a storm; a fountain frothing
where children wade, illegally, to douse
themselves and pick up quarters with their toes;
a portrait cut to fit a locket. Love
adores itself. Whoever frets and stews
about its passing is a fugitive,
loving the drawn-out hours of apprehension—
thin wind in the maples, avenues hushed,
a sheaf of rough drafts weighted by a basin
of iced tea spiked with vodka. Even a lush,
abashed, should know—you *must* supply the dead,
loading their sun boats, clicking your worry beads.

Matinee

Where is the hum of summer? When will zoos
revive the Carolina parakeet
and generate new species? In what disguise
do angels mill about us in the street
where fruits glow, canopied, arrayed in bins?
How will we know the password when an agent
nudges us in the movie house, from whence
we burst exuberant, rejoicing, urgent
as the flashing waterfall we spent two hours
scrutinizing—the close-ups and the cuts,
freeze-frames of torrid pastures and lush tiers,
fragments of nature, vast sets, panning shots
that churn us to dissolves? Who will emerge,
absent from work, gone since midmorning, changed?

Right-of-Way

1.

The fuel that seems inert—a load of stones
pickaxed in deep mines, dumped from wooden tipples
surrounded by black dust—was once alive.

Fire catches on the vegetative chunks
of high-flame coal that tumbled down a chute
into the tender, where a fireman plunges
his shovel, lifts and swivels toward the cab,
tossing the load into a blazing firebox.

At night, when riding in the cupola
of a caboose, you see a reddish glow
above the boxcars when the firebox door
springs open. Then it's dark, a chilly breeze
blowing the coal smoke through the open window.

2.

The passengers and crew grow meditative
as lamps and stove light magnify the darkness
pressing against the swaying, jerking coach.
They try to gaze beyond their own reflections,
shielding their eyes against the glass, observing
the blur of girders on a steel truss bridge
and blinks of ripples on the creek below.

A dark ridge lounges like a hunting dog
but gives way to a barn, a general store,
a watchman smoking on a warehouse ramp.

3.

Now, though the train is gone, rails sold for scrap,
the ridgeline bristles and the creek still glitters
when fishermen aim a flashlight on the surface.
Hikers can climb the grade on a raised path—
the roadbed of the former right-of-way
where saplings rise from beggarweed and gravel—
and sit on the stone bulkhead of a bridge
that isn't there, not even as a ghost,
just emptiness that's found itself again.

Natural History

In the storefront of Maxilla & Mandible,
the skull and neck bones of a giraffe rise up
    above cactus and milkweed pods.
Fresh from the Natural History Museum,
    I'm on my way to a vacant lot,
        a stretch of garden, the Rock 'n' Roll
Memorial Estate, rife with Johnny Jump-Up
    and Never-Die, cast-iron headboards
for decoration, and seats from the tops of pillars.

When I first came upon it, I thought of dark hours
practicing with my band. Plugged in, I thumbed
    the thick strings of a bass and crooned
backup with my choirboy voice. We cut a record
    in a row-house studio, dragging
        amps and drums up a narrow staircase.
The pianist had to play a broken-down upright
    in the basement, connected to
the engineer's glassed-in booth with crackly headphones.

        But here, now, the sign's
          gone, dead stars unnamed,
    missing, a willow swelling in the middle
and roses in bloom, the garden enduring
        despite the city's jamming
with taxi horns, banged garbage cans,
        the only remnant

   of its dedication to hot pop sounds
on the back wall: "RAP," spray-painted in green.
    It might as well be RIP.

Where are the soul singers, glowing in gold lamé?
Where are the growlers, the soothsayers who rocked hard
  in basements, burning to master
all that perishes to a hell-bent backbeat?
  Where's Denise, the folk-rocker, who tripped
  through English class? Where's Rick, who boasted
he'd kill himself by thirty? Where's Kim, lead guitar,
  who raped a girl who'd passed out drunk?
Where's Sheldon, the organist, with his genius IQ?

Once there were lovely names like Lennon and Marley,
sweet to say aloud, and the swaying of reggae,
  incense for torrid city nights.
But even the city of the dead comes to ruin.
  If we're lucky, the vegetation
  will cover up everything we've muffed
and botched. If we're lucky, we can dance out late
  around nothing, like ancient
celebrants in a dying and outrageous cult.

   When I walk home, now,
    I watch ailanthus shoots
  gaining a purchase on rubble and debris,
  "stink trees" with spongy wood if you cut them,
    but they needle up through cracks,

up grates, from edges of buildings,
        while a boom box fades
      and everything sweetens like Eden
for a moment—all we get. Already, the trees
        of heaven are taking over.

JOHN PHILIP DRURY is the author of three previous books of poetry: *The Refugee Camp* (Turning Point Books, 2011), *Burning the Aspern Papers* (Miami University Press, 2003), and *The Disappearing Town* (Miami University Press, 2000). He has also written *The Poetry Dictionary* and *Creating Poetry*, both published by Writer's Digest Books. His awards include a Pushcart Prize, two Ohio Arts Council grants, an Ingram Merrill Foundation fellowship, and the Bernard F. Conners Prize from *The Paris Review*. He is a Professor of English at the University of Cincinnati.

Photo by Jonathan Kamholtz

Also from Able Muse Press

William Baer, *Times Square and Other Stories*

Melissa Balmain, *Walking in on People – Poems*

Ben Berman, *Strange Borderlands – Poems*

Michael Cantor, *Life in the Second Circle – Poems*

Catherine Chandler, *Lines of Flight – Poems*

William Conelly, *Uncontested Grounds – Poems*

Maryann Corbett, *Credo for the Checkout Line in Winter – Poems*

D.R. Goodman, *Greed: A Confession – Poems*

Margaret Ann Griffiths, *Grasshopper – The Poetry of M A Griffiths*

Ellen Kaufman, *House Music – Poems*

Carol Light, *Heaven from Steam – Poems*

April Lindner, *This Bed Our Bodies Shaped – Poems*

Martin McGovern, *Bad Fame – Poems*

Jeredith Merrin, *Cup – Poems*

Richard Newman, *All the Wasted Beauty of the World – Poems*

Frank Osen, *Virtue, Big as Sin – Poems*

Alexander Pepple (Editor), *Able Muse Anthology*

Alexander Pepple (Editor), *Able Muse – a review of poetry, prose & art* (semiannual issues, Winter 2010 onward)

James Pollock, *Sailing to Babylon – Poems*

Aaron Poochigian, *The Cosmic Purr – Poems*

Stephen Scaer, *Pumpkin Chucking – Poems*

Hollis Seamon, *Corporeality – Stories*

Matthew Buckley Smith, *Dirge for an Imaginary World – Poems*

Barbara Ellen Sorensen, *Compositions of the Dead Playing Flutes – Poems*

Wendy Videlock, *The Dark Gnu and Other Poems*

Wendy Videlock, *Nevertheless – Poems*

Wendy Videlock, *Slingshots and Love Plums – Poems*

Richard Wakefield, *A Vertical Mile – Poems*

Chelsea Woodard, *Vellum – Poems*

www.ablemusepress.com

www.ingramcontent.com/pod-product-compliance
Lightning Source LLC
Chambersburg PA
CBHW030122170426
43198CB00009B/707